Original title:
Peppermint Kisses and Sugarplum Wishes

Copyright © 2024 Creative Arts Management OÜ
All rights reserved.

Author: Kieran Blackwood
ISBN HARDBACK: 978-9916-90-876-1
ISBN PAPERBACK: 978-9916-90-877-8

A Symphony of Sugarstorms

Snowflakes tumble, oh what a sight,
Gumdrops dancing, pure delight.
Chocolate rivers, flowing wide,
Candy canes, we cannot hide.

A marshmallow moon, so fluffy and bright,
Sipping hot cocoa, feels just right.
Sprinkles rain down, a colorful cheer,
We'll munch on sweets, till the new year!

Frosty noses, and giggles galore,
With lollipop laughter, who could ask for more?
Strawberry dreams in a cotton candy swirl,
Every day is a berry-fun whirl!

Jingle bells ringing, the snowmen dance,
In this sugar-coated, whimsical trance.
Oh what fun, let our spirits soar,
This frosty fiesta, we'll all adore!

Whirling Hearts Beneath Winter's Veil

Underneath the frosty star,
Gingerbread men dash from afar.
Frosting trails, a sugary spree,
Winter nights filled with glee.

Sledding downs and cookie fights,
Chasing shadows in winter's whites.
Fa-la-la's fill the crisp night air,
With every giggle, without a care.

Twinkling lights like fireflies glow,
Laughter dances in the snow.
Sipping on cider, a cinnamon treat,
With each sip, our hearts skip a beat!

Snowmen waltz in silly poses,
While licorice lamps light our noses.
Funky sweaters with reindeer cheer,
In this funny season, let's spread the cheer!

The Magic of Sweet Delights

In a world where candy rains,
Lollipops dance on sugar trains.
Gumdrops giggle, jellybeans hop,
A candy kingdom, never stop!

Chocolate rivers swirl and flow,
Marshmallow clouds put on a show.
With jelly roll trees and syrup streams,
The sweetest place to chase your dreams.

Songs of Sweetness in Silent Nights

Under the moon, the cookies sing,
Cupcakes twirl, and candy's bling.
Sprinkles rain down, so colorful,
In sugar-coated nights, so wonderful!

Frosting fights and candy canes,
Balloons filled with sour pains.
With giggles echoing in the air,
Sweetened breezes, without a care.

Cocoa Wishes and Frosted Whims

Wishing on a chocolate star,
With frosted dreams, we'll go so far.
Cocoa rivers fuel our fire,
With whipped cream dreams, we'll never tire!

Cookie sprinkles on our toes,
Jollity in every dose.
We'll skate on fudge and slide on cream,
In our sugary, sweetened dream.

Enchanted Flavors in Chill's Embrace

In chilly lands where candies grow,
Marzipan snowflakes twist and flow.
With glee, we taste each frosty treat,
In this whimsical, fun-filled feat!

Luminous lollies light the way,
In a frosty dance, we play.
Giggling elves in candy coats,
Silly jingles, sweetly wrote.

Winter's Sweet Embrace

Snowflakes tumble down like clowns,
Tickling noses, wearing silly frowns.
Hot cocoa spills, what a wild sight,
Don't drink it fast, or you'll take flight!

Scarves wrapped tight, we strut and prance,
Like penguins slipping in a goofy dance.
With each joyful laugh and snowball thrown,
We're children again, in winter's zone!

Candyfloss Dreams in Frosty Air

Fluffy clouds of sugar spin so bright,
Tickling your taste buds with pure delight.
Frostbitten toes in boots too tight,
Who knew winter could feel so light?

Candy canes twirl in a dance so sweet,
Elves with giggles scamper from their seat.
Sugar sprinkles rain down like snow,
Making us all a bit too slow!

Whispers of Sugared Joy

Giggling kids with cheeks aglow,
Chasing each other but moving slow.
With laughter echoing off the trees,
Winter's charm brings us to our knees.

Frosty breath forms clouds in the air,
While squirrels giggle without a care.
A mishap here, a slip or two,
Makes each moment feel brand new!

Frosted Delights and Frostbite Serenades

Frosted windows hide a silly crew,
Making faces with an icy hue.
Snowmen with top hats wobble and sway,
As laughter leads us into play.

Hot cider spills on the snow-white ground,
With every sip, goofiness is found.
Comical slips, trips, and falls abound,
In this winter circus all around!

Sweet Echoes of the Slumbering Season

Winter whispers with a grin,
Chasing snowflakes with a spin.
Socks slip-slide on icy floors,
Laughter bursts through open doors.

Chill in the air, a giggle spree,
Sipping cocoa, feeling glee.
Marshmallows floating, a sweet delight,
Sugar-coated dreams take flight.

Memories Made of Frosted Dreams

Snowmen laugh with carrot noses,
As fluffy flakes upon them dozes.
Snowball fights in frosty cheer,
Chasing giggles, winter's here!

Frosted panes like art on glass,
Drifting wishes, let them pass.
Candy canes in hand held high,
Sweet remembrances float nearby.

Sought After Surprises in a Winter's Tale

Tinsel twinkles, whispers bright,
Surprises hide in soft moonlight.
Shiny ribbons dance and sway,
Beneath the tree where wishes lay.

Mittens mismatched, oh what fun,
Chasing shadows, everyone!
Gifts wrapped tight, not what they seem,
Tickled fancy, waking dreams.

The Crunch of Frosty Footsteps

Crunchy paths on snowy ground,
Echo laughter all around.
Boots that squish, oh what a sound,
Smiles abound where joy is found.

Frosty noses, cheeks so red,
Waddling ducks, let's feed some bread.
Winter's chill, but hearts are warm,
In cozy clothes, we brave the storm.

Glimmering Sweetness Under Starlight

In the pantry, cookies gleam,
A chocolate chip drips like a dream.
Marshmallow fluff takes a dive,
While gingerbread men come alive!

Sprinkling sugar, oh what a sight,
Frosting battles, laughter in flight.
A cookie crunch here, a giggle there,
Uneaten sweets make a fine affair!

A Dance of Frost and Flavor

A snowflake lands on a pie so bright,
Dance of crunch in a frosty bite.
Icicles dangle like candy canes,
While fruitcake sings and joy remains!

Lollipops spin like a twirling tree,
A sweet parade, come taste with me!
Flavors clash in a merry whirl,
As jellybeans twirl in a joyful swirl!

Jingle Bells in a Candy Realm

Jingle bells ring, but do they sing?
Perhaps they laugh, or do weird things.
Fudge brick roads lead to gumdrop hills,
Choco rivers bring giggles and thrills!

Marzipan castles glimmer and shine,
While candy canes play hopscotch in line.
The licorice trees sway to the beat,
As gummy bears dance, oh what a treat!

The Scent of Spices and Wonder

Cinnamon sprinkles on noses abound,
With nutmeg whispers, sweetness is found.
The cookie jar giggles as it hides,
While chocolate truffles bounce and glide!

Cakes hold secrets of frosting delight,
While caramel rivers flow warm at night.
Bakers twirl in a floury dream,
As cupcakes giggle, how sweet they seem!

The Lightness of Gingerbread Echoes

In the kitchen, flour flies,
Ginger men dance, oh what a surprise!
Frosting smiles and candy frowns,
Joyful chaos in our towns.

Rolling pins become a sword,
Fighting crumbs in one accord.
Baking tales that never end,
With icing swirls, we all pretend.

Glimpses of Delight Through Silver Snow

The snowflakes fall like tiny hats,
Dancing dogs and chubby cats.
Snowball fights and laughter bright,
Making magic on this night.

Under twinkling lights we cheer,
Sipping cocoa, spreading cheer.
Neighbors peek with noses pressed,
And jump with joy, we're all so blessed!

Rustic Flavors of Cozy Evenings

Chairs pulled close around the fire,
S'mores and stories never tire.
Crackling logs and songbirds sing,
Joyful moments they do bring.

We wear our socks with silly flair,
In our little comfy lair.
Laughter echoes, shadows dance,
Silly pranks lead to romance.

Sweets and Dreams from All Around

Sugary clouds and taffy rain,
Giggles bubble, joy's our gain.
Chocolate rivers flow with glee,
What a wacky jubilee!

Candy canes with stripes so bold,
Whispers of stories yet untold.
In this land, we shout and play,
Tomorrow's sweets will save the day!

A Symphony of Sugar and Snow

In a world of frosted glee,
Sugar sprinkles dance for free.
Snowflakes swirl with giggles bright,
Creating magic in the night.

A candy cane on every tree,
Chirping birds sing happily.
Marshmallow clouds drift overhead,
While gingerbread dreams fill with dread.

Hot cocoa spills on my new shirt,
As powdered snowflakes start to flirt.
Laughter echoes, sweet and light,
In this frosty, joyful plight.

With gumdrops piled in a stack,
We waddle home, but not look back.
The symphony of cold and sweet,
Is where our winter dreams compete.

Sweets Beneath the Mistletoe

Beneath the boughs of green and red,
I found a treat, much to my dread.
A rogue jellybean jumped my way,
And I giggled, 'Oh no!' to my dismay.

With marshmallow fluff in my hair,
I twirl around without a care.
Bound by candy she's got me caught,
In sticky hugs, oh sugary thought.

The chocolate elves have made a mess,
With giggles hard to suppress.
A lollipop dance, so absurdly bright,
Only at merry holiday night!

So when you peek beneath the leaves,
Beware of sweets that pulls and cleaves.
For fun awaits in every kiss,
Right there in jolly, sweet abyss.

Holiday Hues of Honey and Spice

In a kitchen filled with spice and cheer,
I spilled the honey, oh dear, oh dear!
Gingerbread men are on the run,
Tasting treats is all in fun!

Cinnamon squirrels chase around,
As icing frowns, from upside down.
Caramel drips from the rafters high,
While chocolate looks suspiciously shy.

Nutmeg giggles and twirls about,
As cookie monsters roam with clout.
With every bite, a holiday cheer,
The sweetest season of the year.

So grab a treat and take a seat,
Savor flavors, oh what a feat!
In this land where smiles entice,
Join the fun of honey and spice!

Glimmering Joys on Snowy Evenings

As snowflakes twinkle in the light,
We build a snowman, quite the sight.
Carrot nose and buttons of coal,
In winter wonderland, we feel whole.

With doughnut hats and popsicle arms,
He waves hello with quirky charms.
Beneath the glow of streetlamp's glow,
We laugh and dance in the evening snow.

Candy sleighs race by with glee,
While licorice whips take a spree.
With each slip and slide, oh so bold,
There's magic here, if truth be told.

So gather 'round with sweets in hand,
Join the laughter in this wonderland.
Glimmering joys, so sweet and bright,
Fill snowy evenings with pure delight.

Frosted Hopes in Holiday Glow

In a world of laughter, we wear our glee,
Sipping hot cocoa, oh what a spree!
Sugar sprinkles dance on our tongues,
As we giggle and hum merry old songs.

Gingerbread men with frosting smiles,
Chase after us for endless miles.
Marshmallow clouds float in the air,
Sweet childhood dreams, beyond compare.

The Flavors of Frost

Flavors collide in a jolly swirl,
Candy canes spin, watch them twirl.
Chocolate giggles and vanilla delight,
Together they party all through the night.

Frosty delights and fruity cheer,
Nibbling on sweets, let's shed a tear.
Not of sadness, but joy to behold,
As we unwrap the stories retold.

Tinsel and Twinkle

Glitter shines from every nook,
Baking up trouble, let's take a look!
Ornament balls bouncing around,
Laughter erupts with each silly sound.

Tinsel fights with the cat for fame,
While the dog joins in, igniting the game.
Christmas lights twinkle, stars start to wink,
All in good humor, let's raise a drink!

Snowflakes on Sugarcoated Hearts

Snowflakes fall like whimsical jokes,
Tickling noses of giggling folks.
Hearts wrapped in laughter, sweetened with cheer,
Sipping fond memories with those we hold dear.

Will the snowmen rise or melt away?
With carrot noses, will they sway?
Frosty dances, a whimsical art,
Laughter's the glue on sugarcoated hearts.

Sugary Echoes of Yuletide Cheer

In the kitchen, pans a-jingle,
Flour flies as we stir and mingle.
A dash of chaos, a sprinkle of fun,
   Cookies shaped like everyone!

Laughter spills like melted fudge,
A recipe read with a cheeky grudge.
Gingerbread men with silly grins,
Who knew baking could lead to wins?

Mismatched socks, and sprinkles galore,
Sugar highs make us dance on the floor.
Eggnog quips shared with glee,
   What's sweeter than this jubilee?

So let the holiday giggles soar,
With candy hearts and tales galore.
As we toast with milk and cookies near,
   Here's to joyous, sugary cheer!

Lullabies draped in Candy Cane Stripes

A snore from the couch, the dog takes flight,
Chasing dreams of red stripes in the night.
Whispers of chocolate and joyful trips,
While twinkling lights dance and flip.

Santa's reindeer, they start to zoom,
In the kitchen, a mischievous broom!
Sugarplum fairies hide in the glow,
Wishing all sweet dreams, on the go!

Elves in a tangle with wrapping bows,
Giggles escape as mischief grows.
Cocoa cups spill over in cheers,
As laughter chases away the fears.

In pajamas, we lounge, then jump with glee,
Creating more chaos under the tree.
With candy dreams wrapped tight at night,
We'll laugh 'til dawn, in pure delight.

Dreaming in Frost and Confection

Frosty windows, a cake pops' glee,
Snowflakes swirl, come play with me.
Marshmallow pillows cushion our falls,
As laughter echoes through the halls.

Cupcake towers sway and tip,
With colorful icing from every trip.
Sugar-coated clouds on a midnight ride,
Chasing giggles 'neath the starry tide.

Whiskers twitch, a cat in disguise,
Hints of frosting in those wide eyes.
A spoon in hand, ready to dive,
Let's eat until we feel alive!

With dreams that bubble like fizzy drinks,
Our hearts are light, don't you think?
In a world spun fast, we laugh and cheer,
In sugary dreams, we hold so dear.

Sweet Spice waltzes through the Snow

With a twirl, the cinnamon rolls unfold,
Tales of sweet mischief are boldly told.
Pine cones wrapped like gifts of cheer,
   Snowmen snickering year after year.

Frosty air and gingerbread hats,
Squirrels stealing treats, imagine that!
Laughter 'n giggles in the cold,
An annual dance that never gets old.

A peppermint twist in a woolly scarf,
Creating snow angels while we laugh.
With each bumbling step in the snow,
The fun never stops, just see how we glow!

So we waltz on frosty avenues,
Sipping cocoa, sharing our views.
In a whimsical spin, we gather 'round,
In sweetness and chuckles, love is found.

Sweets for the Snowbound Soul

When snowflakes fall and giggles rise,
A snowman wears a doughnut guise.
With frosting arms and jellybean eyes,
He's got a sweet tooth, oh what a surprise!

The kids are stuck, but they don't mind,
Sugar rush is what they find.
In snowball battles, candy blinds,
With lollipop shields, their joy unwinds!

They twirl and spin, the world is bright,
Attempting to fly on marshmallow flight.
But gravity wins; it's quite a sight,
As gummy bears giggle in delight!

So here's to snow with flavors sweet,
A frozen feast, a snowy treat.
With each frosty bite, joy's complete,
In a wonderland where fun and sweets meet.

Magic Spun in Candy Floss

In a carnival whirl of bright delight,
Spun sugar clouds take glorious flight.
A laughter-filled mix, oh what a sight,
As children giggle, no end in sight!

With sticky hands and faces smeared,
They dance on toes, unbothered, cheered.
Flavors swirl, and stress disappears,
Magic in each sugary sneer!

Taffy pulls and caramel dreams,
Life's more fun with double-dipped creams.
In this candy land, joy beams,
Where laughter pops like soda streams!

So taste the rainbow, let worries drop,
In sugary realms that never stop.
With giggles that astound and hop,
In this twirly world, it's never a flop!

Dreams Entwined with Frosted Ferns

Where winter whispers among the trees,
Frosted ferns dance in the chilly breeze.
They weave sweet dreams with sugary ease,
While chocolate petals drift with glee!

The fairies sip hot cocoa at night,
Spinning stardust to sweeten delight.
With marshmallow pillows, they laugh and write,
A tale of joy that's out of sight!

Each flake that falls is a sprinkle of cheer,
A frosty giggle as they come near.
With ticklish toes, they have no fear,
In sweet dreams spun, the world's a sphere!

So let's float away on fluffy clouds,
In a dreamy land that's fun and loud.
With candy forests and laughter proud,
Our frosted ferns shall wear a shroud!

Sugar and Spice Beneath the Pines

Beneath the pines where snowdrifts lay,
A gingerbread house leads the playful fray.
With licorice ropes to show the way,
And marshmallow clouds where children play!

The cinnamon smells mix with winter's chill,
Creating a scene that's fun to thrill.
Peppered giggles up on the hill,
As they build sweet forts, laughter can't still!

In sugar-coated dreams, all's a gleam,
Childhood's joy, the sweetest theme.
With cookies and tales that kindly redeem,
Fun awaits in every sugary beam!

So come along, bring your candy flair,
In this winter wonder, we'll laugh and share!
With sugar and spice, there's magic in the air,
A jolly romp, in delight we'll care!

Glimmering Shores of Mirth

On sandy shores where giggles play,
Seagulls dance in a silly sway.
With laughter mixed in salty air,
We build our castles without a care.

A crab in shades of neon green,
Winks at us, so bold, so keen.
We chase him down, it's quite a feat,
While tripping on our sandy feet.

The sun's a jester, bright and round,
With golden jokes that all abound.
We tumble over waves so grand,
With joy, forever hand in hand.

Never a frown, just sunny grins,
With sonnets sung by playful winds.
In this mirthful world, let us play,
And chase those giggles through the day.

Candlelight Fables of Invite

Candlelight dances, shadows tease,
The table's set with playful ease.
A dinner guest with socks askew,
Chomps on a roll, and oh, how he blew!

Stories spun with silly flair,
Of talking chairs and polka bears.
We sip our drinks, a splash or two,
As laughter echoes, 'What's your shoe?'

Fables told of beasts and pies,
And a lost mouse that wore a guise.
We snicker while the candles drip,
What a night, a joyful trip!

With every wink, a plot unwinds,
The jests grow wild, like tangled vines.
So gather close, dear friends, unite,
In candlelight, where dreams take flight.

Festive Flavors and Fiery Hues

A pot of stew that jumps with cheer,
Sings a tune that we all hear.
With spices dancing, oh, so bold,
A spoonful's tale is fun retold.

Tinsel twinkles in jolly hue,
While cookies sprout with eyes askew.
The oven puffs with a fruity grin,
As gingerbread folks begin to spin.

A pie that croons a custard song,
While lollipop trees sway all day long.
Each bite's a burst of zany glee,
With jellybeans roaming wild and free.

In kitchens bright with festal flare,
We laugh and sing without a care.
So ladle out those zesty fun,
For flavors dance, we've only just begun!

Whimsies and Delights Amidst the Chill

Outside the frost begins to play,
With snowy antics on display.
A snowman sporting a silly grin,
Winks at us as the fun begins.

We toss the snow, it somehow flies,
To land on cats with silly sighs.
While penguins slide with clumsy grace,
In a merry race, it's such a chase!

Hot cocoa flows like bubbling streams,
With marshmallow fluff that's fit for dreams.
We cozy by the fire's crackle light,
Telling jokes that tickle all night.

So bundle up, let laughter spill,
Amidst the chill, we find the thrill.
In winter's whimsy, we shall bask,
With frosty mirth, it's all we ask!

Tinsel and Taffy

Tinsel twirls on the tree, oh so bright,
Kids are sneaking treats late at night.
Gumdrops giggle as they fall,
Candy canes try to dance, but trip and sprawl.

Elves are baking with their cheeky grins,
Flour flies like snow, where the fun begins.
Marshmallows jump in hot cocoa baths,
While gingerbread men calculate their paths.

a Festive Affair

A snowman in sunglasses, what a sight,
With a scarf that's too long, snugged up tight.
Jingle bells ringing, all out of tune,
As cats chase ribbons beneath the moon.

Chocolates laugh as they melt and swirl,
In the kitchen, flour is flying like a whirl.
Stockings are stuffed with socks and glee,
Children wonder if Santa loves brie.

Starry Nights and Sugared Sights

Stars are winking from above with flair,
While reindeer practice yoga in mid-air.
Candles flicker like they're doing the twist,
Nutcracker soldiers can't resist a tryst.

Snowflakes dance in a flurry of fun,
Each one a story, a tale to run.
This joyful chaos brings laughter and cheer,
With a pie on the window saying, "Come here!"

Lollipops Dancing in the Winter Breeze

Lollipops are looping in the chilly night,
Seagulls in hats are ready for a bite.
Icicles jingle like wind chimes so rare,
As sugar plums prance in the frosty air.

Fudge is fighting for room on a plate,
While cupcakes giggle at their sugary fate.
Brownies just wink, doing all the tricks,
In this candy land, there's joy in the mix.

Frosty Treats and Dreamy Feats

Frosty treats in a sugar-bound race,
Gingerbread houses keep losing their place.
Marzipan mice sneak in for a munch,
While kids gather 'round for their sweet little lunch.

A penguin with shades slides on sweet cream,
With a cherry on top, it's a whimsical dream.
Snowballs put sprinkles, just for some fun,
At this winter feast, there's laughter for everyone.

Glazed Surprises Wrapped in Love

In a jar of sweet delight,
Cookies dance with pure delight,
Sprinkles flying everywhere,
Who knew sugar could be a scare?

A donut's glazed with a giggle,
Lollipops make everyone wiggle,
Chocolate drizzles on my nose,
Can't help but strike a silly pose!

Frosting fights and cupcake wars,
Silly things that lighten chores,
Sweets may burst right from their seams,
Who needs sleep when we have dreams?

Wrapped in love and frosted cheer,
Chocolate-covered laughs appear,
Every bite's a funny song,
In our sugary world, we belong!

Cocoa Clouds and Sugary Stars

Cocoa clouds float so high,
Marshmallows drift and sigh,
With each sip, a silly sound,
Giggles from the cocoa mound.

Stars made of candy glare,
Laughter fills the frosty air,
Sipping sweets from giant mugs,
Even snowmen give us hugs!

Frothy mustaches on our face,
Chasing laughs at a sweet pace,
Lollipops that twirl and twine,
Who knew sugar could be divine?

In this world of blissful treats,
Giggles bloom and joy repeats,
So let the laughter swirl around,
In cocoa dreams, we are found!

The Cheer Beneath the Mistletoe

Beneath the sprig, we dance and twirl,
Cotton candy makes us swirl,
With every giggle in the air,
Kisses float, sweet moments share.

Mistletoe with a gummy twist,
Sweets and laughs that coexist,
Chocolates hide in festive bows,
Who knew love could taste like those?

Tickled toes in winter's light,
With each chuckle, hearts ignite,
Jellybeans in snowflakes fall,
Wrapped in cheer, we have it all!

With sugary wishes, hugs abound,
Underneath that mistletoe mound,
Every sweet is full of zest,
In laughter's warmth, we feel the best!

Celestial Confections of Winter's Embrace

Under stars, the treats fall down,
Sugar snowflakes twirl around,
Giggles echo in the night,
Chocolate moons, a silly sight.

Cotton clouds of whipped cream dream,
Bubbles burst with laughter's beam,
Dancing spoons with cinnamon flair,
Every bite, a sweet treasure rare!

Caramel rivers, candy canes,
Frosting floods like sugar rains,
Lollipop kisses on our cheeks,
Sweetest laughter is what peaks!

In winter's warm, we find our glee,
Beneath the stars, just you and me,
Celestial sweets and merry grace,
In sugary hugs, we find our place!

Cherry Sweetness in Twilight's Glow

Under candy skies, we twirl and spin,
Laughing at the gumdrops, all sticky with grin.
Cherry-flavored giggles burst in the air,
As we chase the choco-rabbits without any care.

Lollipops waving, they twirl with delight,
While sugar plums play hide and seek at night.
We build a sweet fortress made of bright glee,
Tasting each moment of frosty jubilee.

Jellybean rain falls, bright colors collide,
With sprinkles of laughter, there's no need to hide.
In this land of whimsy, our worries dissolve,
Surrounded by sweetness, our hearts can't resolve.

So join in the dance, let your spirit be free,
In this twilight wonder, just you and me.
We'll mix all our joy in a fizzy champagne,
Then bounce off the walls like a sugar-high train.

Marshmallow Clouds and Starry Dreams

Fluffy white pillows float high up in the sky,
We dive in sweet dreams that make our hearts sigh.
Cotton candy whispers wrap round the night,
While giggles and chuckles light up the delight.

Wobbling on marshmallows, we bounce one by one,
Chasing starlit sprinkles, oh what reckless fun!
With chocolate syrup rivers flowing so sweet,
Each dip is a chance for more laughter to meet.

Twirling in the breeze, we taste every star,
Each bite bursting magic from places afar.
Cupcake horizons and gumball trees,
We swing on each whim, fueled by giggly breeze.

As we float on this dream cloud, our fancies take flight,
Making wishes on sprinkles that shine in the night.
Life's a big party with flavors galore,
So come join the fun, who could ask for more?

Glistening Treats Beneath the Moon

Under a bright moon, we nibble and munch,
Glistening goodies, a whimsical brunch.
Fizzy drinks shimmer, swirling with cheer,
As we giggle with joy, there's nothing to fear.

Dancing with pickles and jelly-filled pies,
We jive with the flavors beneath twinkling skies.
Sprinkled confetti falls, a tasty parade,
With laughter as thick as the frosting we made.

Taffy-tongued toasters toast marshmallows high,
With every silly story, we soar and we fly.
We build up our dreams on a cookie-based tower,
Each layer a memory, our own sugary power.

So under the moonlight, let's giggle and play,
With treats all around, we'll savor the day.
In this land of sweet whimsy, our hearts will take flight,
For life is a banquet of laughter tonight!

Sugary Joyrides through Winter's Bliss

Zooming on sleds made of candy cane twirls,
We dash through the frost, where sweetness unfurls.
Giggles and snowflakes twirl all around,
In this sugary wonderland, joy is profound.

Sprinkled with laughter from noses to toes,
We chase snowy flakes with our marshmallow bows.
Each smile is a treat that we share in the fun,
As we slide down the slopes beneath winter's sun.

With licorice laughter and sparkles of cheer,
We soar on candy clouds, feeling no fear.
Our hearts race like chocolate, so pure and so bright,
In this magical winter, it feels just right.

So grab your sweet friends for a gleeful ride,
Through a wintery landscape where we all collide.
In this blissful adventure, hold on tight, you'll see,
For every bite of joy lasts for eternity!

Sparkling Embers of Yuletide

We gather round with mugs in hand,
With marshmallows floating like tiny land.
The cat steals the cookies, what a sight!
We're laughing so hard, it's pure delight.

The tree lights blink like they're in a race,
Or are they just trying to change their pace?
Grandma's fruitcake, a mystery still,
We eye it closely, then eat our fill.

Uncle Joe's stories, they never get old,
He swears there's a ghost that once stole the gold.
The laughter erupts, oh what a crew,
We'll always embrace our odd little brew.

So here's to the moments we cherish the most,
With giggles and snacks, we'll raise up a toast!
Through the chaos and fun, we find our cheer,
In sparkling embers, we hold each year!

Glazed Dreams Through Snowy Scenes

The snowflakes swirl like performers on cue,
While I'm out here, slipping like a shoe!
My gingerbread house looks a bit askew,
But oh, what a treat when I bite into blue!

Hot cocoa spills, a chocolaty mess,
My mittens are stuck, oh what a stress!
John's wearing jammies with snowmen galore,
It's tough to take him seriously anymore.

The snowman's scarf, it's a sight to behold,
All mismatched patterns, both brash and bold.
He stands there proud, gives a cheeky wave,
While I dodge the snowballs my friends misbehave!

Through frosty adventures, we giggle and glide,
With glazed dreams and snow, we take it in stride.
Each moment we share is a treasure, you see,
In the snowy fun, we all long to be free!

Nostalgic Nibbles of the Past

We munch on treats from back in our youth,
Like candy canes shaped into a tooth!
Mom's no-bake cookies, a legend, they say,
We argue over recipes, come what may.

The fruitcake's shining like a disco ball,
We take a small bite, and we cautiously crawl.
Remember those candies all sticky and sweet?
We'll dare each other, then laugh at our feet.

The joy of these nibbles, a twist of good fun,
Like catching the laughter under the sun.
From chewy to crunchy, they dance on our tongue,
Who knew that nostalgia feels so young?

In the end, it's the joy that binds us tight,
Through bites and giggles, everything feels right.
With nostalgic nibbles and cheeky grins,
We'll keep this tradition as laughter begins!

Fragrant Frosted Moments

The oven's roaring, a festive delight,
With cookies that disappear in one bite.
Flour clouds swirl like a busy snowstorm,
In our kitchen chaos, the laughter is warm.

The frosting's a rainbow, a colorful mess,
We start a cream fight, oh what a stress!
With sprinkles flying like a confetti blast,
We'll take on the day, here's hoping it lasts!

Uncle Bob's dancing with a spatula high,
While Grandma rolls dough, she can really fly!
Each moment is fragrant, with giggles abound,
In this frosted wonderland, joy can be found.

So let's raise a spoon to these silly old times,
Where laughter and sweetness blend into rhymes.
Through fragrant frosted moments we share,
In this giddy chaos, we'll always find care!

Dreams Dusted with Sweetness

In a land where candy grows,
Each dream comes sweetly, don't you know?
Chocolates dance and cookies sing,
With every bite, a little zing!

Marshmallow clouds that float on by,
Sticky fingers wave hello, oh my!
Lollipop trees in vibrant hues,
Tickle your taste, spread sweetened news!

Giggles echo as sprinkles rain,
A frosty breeze stirs up the fun again,
Candy canes with hearts so bright,
Dreams of treats that feel just right!

So join the feast, let laughter soar,
In this land of sweets, we want more!
With every giggle, bite, and laugh,
We find joy in the sugar path!

The Magic of Minty Moments

In minty moments, joy is found,
With silly smiles and laughs abound.
Wobbling like jelly, we prance with glee,
Tasting wonders, just you and me!

Sipping cocoa with marshmallow fluff,
Every sip feels just so tough.
Watch sugar critters put on a show,
They twirl and twist, putting on a glow!

Candied laughter fills the air,
As minty breath spreads love and care.
We chase the giggles, spin around,
In this jolly place, pure fun is found!

So grab a sweet, come join the fun,
In minty moments, we leap and run!
A sprinkle of joy, a dash of cheer,
In this magical world, we hold dear!

Frostbite and Fondness

With icy toes and laughter bright,
We dance through snowflakes, pure delight.
Frostbite bites, but smiles grow wide,
We navigate this whimsical ride!

Snowmen chat with carrot noses,
Sharing jokes as the chilly wind dozes.
Frosty breath creates a theater,
Where humor melts away the bitter!

Hot cocoa spills, oh what a sight,
Whipped cream clouds that take to flight.
With every sip, we cheer and tease,
In this winter wonderland, we freeze!

So wrap up warm, don your cap,
Join in the fun, who needs a nap?
With frostbite's chill and fondness glows,
We chuckle through the winter snows!

Holiday Delights Wrapped in Cheer

In the season of giving, we wrap it bold,
Delights that shine like treasures of gold.
With giggles and games, the laughter flows,
Each gift we open, a surprise that glows!

Cookies frosted with silly designs,
A sprinkle mishap that perfectly shines.
Candy canes twirling in mock ballet,
Let's jump, sing, and dance all day!

Presents pile high, what will it be?
The joy of surprise is plain to see.
With each unwrapping, we bust out loud,
Holiday cheer that swells up the crowd!

So let's cherish this festive spell,
With giggles and sweets that taste so well.
In holiday delight wrapped in fun,
Together we'll laugh till the year is done!

Wishes Wrapped in Sweet Surrender

A jolly old elf with a belly so round,
Dances in circles without making a sound.
His pockets are full of sweets in a mess,
He trades them for giggles, oh what a success!

Those dreams made of fudge, piled high like a hill,
Turn every child's mouth into a chocolate mill.
With sprinkles and spritzers, no need to hold back,
We'll feast on our wishes from every bright sack.

In candy-coated worlds where the gumdrops grow,
The reindeer debate whether to fly or to tow.
With laughter and sugar, our hearts light and spry,
We'll swap all our secrets as the snowflakes fly!

So come join the party with cupcakes to bake,
The more that we giggle, the less we will ache.
In this land of sweetness, let worries take flight,
For wishes wrapped up make the cold nights feel bright.

Candied Dreams and Winter Whispers

In a cozy café with treats piled high,
A squirrel in a sweater keeps passing by.
He snags a cookie, but runs with a pout,
The frosting's too sticky, oh what's this about?

There's hot cocoa bubbling with marshmallows peeking,
While snowflakes are singing and children are squeaking.

They build frosty giants with noses that drip,
As they giggle and wiggle with candy to sip.

The gingerbread houses are wobbly, oh dear!
One dog made a dash, now it's really unclear.
With icing on faces and laughter so loud,
Those dreams full of candy make us all feel proud!

So grab all the sprinkles, we're mixing it right,
With gumdrops and laughter, we'll dance through the night.
In this whimsical wonder of sugar and cheer,
Each moment a treat that we hold oh so dear.

Sweet Whispers of Winter Nights

On snowy white nights when the stars seem to play,
There's laughter escaping as friends shout hooray!
With scarves all askew and mittens on tight,
We'll slide down the hill till we've giggled with fright.

The cocoa flows freely, and cookies abound,
While snowmen, with carrots, stand proudly around.
They hold chatty secrets, their voices so deep,
While moonlight keeps watch on the dreams that we keep.

Marshmallows get tossed like soft snowflakes in air,
As children burst onward, their movements with flair.
A sprinkle of chaos, a drizzle of fun,
In this land of sweet whispers, we all feel like one.

So raise up your glasses to toast to this night,
With laughter and cheer, everything feels so right.
For every small snicker and sugary tease,
These moments of joy put our hearts at ease.

Candy Canes and Cozy Dreams

In a parlor where giggles bounce off every wall,
A cat in a hat thinks he's reigning over all.
With candy canes dangling from ears that are fluffed,
He leaps for the table, all sugary and tough.

We hang shiny ornaments, jingle bells ring,
While the sprightly old dog starts to dance and to sing.
With wonders of jelly and taffy so bright,
Every dreamy idea ignites pure delight.

The stockings are empty, but not for long,
We'll fill them with laughter, where all of us belong.
With giggles of joy mixed with frosting on lips,
We dream up a story with adorable quips.

So gather around, and let's share all our treats,
With games, songs, and laughter, we'll make merry feats.

In this cozy delight, wrapped snug as a dream,
We'll savor each moment, delicious and cream.

A Tasty Tale of Joy

In a land where sweets never fade,
Chocolate rivers in bright parade,
Gumdrops dance under the sun,
Lollipops laughing, oh what fun!

Candy canes twist in the breeze,
Sugar sprites giggle with ease,
Frosting castles, so lovely and sweet,
Munchkin munchers skip on warm treats!

Licorice logs roll down the hill,
Bubbly giggles, a thrill to fulfill,
Jellybean jumpers leap so high,
Sprinkled laughter fills the sky!

With every bite, a story unfolds,
Tales of sweetness that never grows old,
Come join the feast, don't be shy,
For joy is served, oh my, oh my!

Bubbles of Bliss on a Winter's Eve

Snowflakes twirl like icing spun,
Giggles frolic, oh what fun!
Cupcake clouds in the moonlight glow,
Dance with marshmallows, moving slow.

Chilly winds bring a frosty cheer,
The aroma of baked goods draws near,
Sipping cocoa, warmth in a wink,
Bubbles of bliss, oh, don't you think?

Tickled tongues taste candy canes,
Joyful hearts shout with sweet refrains,
Squirrels snooze in their cookie homes,
Dreams of sprinkles as night softly roams.

In the starlit sky so bright,
Laughter echoes through the night,
Join in the mirth, let worries cease,
For the magic of sweetness brings peace.

Cheery Chimes and Sweets Divine

Jingle bells ring with a sugary chime,
Lemonade laughter, oh so sublime,
Candy canaries sing in glee,
Tickling toes near the cherry tree.

Nutty dancers swirl all around,
With chocolate notes, a joyful sound,
Cupcakes in crowns, oh what a sight,
Making merry on this starry night.

Sprinkles rain down like colorful cheer,
Each little giggle wraps the year,
Frosty friends with big, pearly grins,
Creating sweet memories, where joy begins.

So grab a treat and join the throng,
For laughter and sweets is where we belong,
With every bite, let gladness take flight,
In a world where everything feels so right!

Seasonal Serenades of Sugar

As winter whispers its frosty tune,
Marzipan mice prance under the moon,
Oh, come one, come all, to the festive fun,
To bounce with joy like a sweet cinnamon bun!

Gingerbread men skip with delight,
While jelly stars shimmer in the night,
Buttercream clouds fluff up the air,
Sprinkled giggles are everywhere.

Lollipops sway in the chilly breeze,
Snowmen chuckle, oh how they tease,
Candied carrots make noses bright,
As sugar sprinkles dance under starlight.

So join the party, don't be late,
In the land of sweets, it's sure to be great,
With joyful hearts in every bite,
Let's celebrate this sugary night!

Glistening Wishes in a Frosty Breeze

Snowflakes tumble from the sky,
As frostbite whispers a playful sigh.
Hot cocoa spills, a marshmallow fight,
Wishing for warmth on this chilly night.

Giggling kids in their winter gear,
Chasing snowmen, spreading cheer.
But wait! What's that? A slippery patch,
Down they go with a comical dispatch!

Winter's chill brings candy canes,
Laughter echoes through frosty plains.
With every slip and twist they find,
Joy and giggles intertwine.

In this frosty realm of delight,
Each glee-filled heart feels so light.
Chasing snowflakes, singing songs,
In the frosty breeze, all laugh along!

A Symphony of Sugary Sights

Sweets parade on festive streets,
Chocolate drizzles and gumdrop treats.
Gingerbread houses stand so tall,
Yet one seems ready to take a fall!

Beneath the lights that shimmer bright,
Candy canes dance in the soft moonlight.
A squirrel jumps and snags a prize,
To the sweet symphony, he replies!

Lollipops twirl in a sugar waltz,
Sweet surprises without any faults.
But oh dear, watch the gumdrops roll,
As everyone dives for their sugary goal!

The laughter echoes through the stalls,
As candies skid and caramel falls.
With every crunch and munch we cheer,
We savor the joy that's always near!

Enchanted Treats of the Season

In a land where treats come alive,
Cookies and sweets in a delightful hive.
Marshmallow clouds float on chocolate streams,
A place where everyone lives their dreams.

Licorice vines twist and twirl,
As candy corn starts to swirl.
Unicorns munch on gumdrop snails,
While sugar sparkles fill the trails.

Glazed donuts wearing winter hats,
Dance with joy — look at those spats!
Candies giggle, cookies tease,
Making mischief with such ease.

So join the fun, don't be late,
Taste the treats that feel so great.
In this enchanted, silly scene,
Every bite is pure and keen!

Cinnamon Stars and Licorice Lights

Stars made of cinnamon twinkle above,
While licorice strands weave tales of love.
In a cookie-filled wonderland we roam,
Searching for sweets that feel like home.

Candy canes hitch a ride on a sleigh,
Flying off into the frosty buffet.
Sprinkles rain down like confetti bright,
As we giggle into the playful night.

The gingerbread men pick up the pace,
In a friendly, sugar-filled race.
Running in circles, they spin and cheer,
Cinnamon is calling — can we steer?

So grab a treat, let's spin around,
In this quirky world, joy will abound.
With laughter and sweets, we'll dance all night,
With cinnamon stars shining so bright!

Wishes on a Candy Cloud

Up above the world so sweet,
Where gummy bears and licorice meet.
Raindrops made of soda pop,
Candy sprites that never stop.

Laughing lollies, dancing bright,
Whirling round in pure delight.
A fizzy breeze that's hard to catch,
With every bite, a silly match.

Sugar bridges made of cream,
Taffy clouds that make you beam.
Soaring high with cookie wings,
In a place where laughter sings.

Just beware of chocolate rain,
For it may cause a giggly strain.
But fear not the sweets that fall,
Embrace the joy, enjoy it all.

Marzipan Moonlight

Underneath the sugar glow,
Marzipan trees begin to grow.
Choco critters in a dance,
Join the merry, frothy prance.

Moonbeams wrapped in caramel,
Swaying sounds from chiming bell.
Starlight twirls in creamy swirls,
As gumdrop flags unfurl.

Cake pop creatures sing their tune,
Beneath a frosted, sugar moon.
Dancing till the morning light,
On marshmallow clouds, oh what a sight!

The jelly stars wink from above,
As laughter fills the air with love.
Join the fun, don't be so shy,
On fluffy meringue, jump up high!

Lollipops Under the Mistletoe

With lollipops hung on the tree,
A twisty surprise waits just for me.
Tickled tongues and sticky grins,
Where every day the fun begins.

Silly stockings filled with sweets,
Dancing near the gumdrop beats.
Candy cane kisses create a fuss,
In a land of joy and sugar plus.

Giggles pop like fizzy drinks,
Merry elves in bright pink clinks.
Caught beneath the sticky sprig,
Double dares make you dance a jig.

Slip on frosting, whoops, oh dear!
But laughter wipes away the fear.
So here's a toast under the glow,
To all the charms that make us grow!

Twirling Through Sugar Snow

In a whirl of fluffy flair,
Sugar snowflakes fill the air.
Twists and turns, we spin around,
Chirpy giggles, joy is found.

Candy canes like ski poles sway,
As we twirl the day away.
Frosted laughter, powdery fun,
Frosty capers, just begun!

Ice cream slides, we glide with ease,
With every scoop, our hearts appease.
Giggling spills, a friendly race,
Through this sweet and dreamy place.

So join the dance, don't hold back,
On sugar paths, we'll stay on track.
Even when the giggles grow,
We'll twirl along through sugar snow!

Comfort in Confectionery Dreams

In a world of chewy delights,
Where gumdrops swirl and dance at night,
Chocolate rivers flow with glee,
Singing songs of candy spree.

Jellybeans jump from jar to jar,
Tickling noses, oh, how bizarre!
Lollipops spin like windmill blades,
Painting smiles in candy parades.

Marshmallow clouds float up so high,
As licorice vines twine and sigh,
Dreams made sweet with sugar's cheer,
Who knew snacks could bring such clear?

Gummy bears wearing tiny hats,
Dancing with cupcakes in sprightly spats,
Let's indulge in this whimsical land,
Where every bite is perfectly planned.

The Joy of Holly and Honey

Under mistletoe we laugh and cheer,
With honey drizzled on toast, oh dear!
Sipping cider with a naughty grin,
We toast to the sweets we can all win.

Gingerbread men with their frosting flair,
Running wild without a care,
Crumbly and giggly, they flee the plate,
Chasing us as we all await.

Tickling taste buds, they make a scene,
Waltzing around like they're on a screen,
The table adorned with treats so bright,
Why yes, I shall have just one more bite!

Honeycomb dreams may buzz and hum,
While giggling glasses of soda come,
We'll savor moments both sweet and funny,
Dancing 'round with our candy money.

Buttercream Wishes in Silver Stars

With a dash of buttercream fun,
Stars twinkle bright, oh what a run!
Frosted cupcakes wear sprinkles proud,
In a bakery bustling with laughter loud.

Sugar plums prance on chocolate streams,
Whisking away all our crazy dreams,
Cookies giggle, all frosted and nice,
Serving joy on a sugary slice.

Nibbled dreams float like marshmallow fluff,
In a confectionery land, never too tough,
Grinning like candy canes on a spree,
The sweetest fun is best with glee!

Frosting fights under starlit nights,
Sweets on the table create such delights,
We'll toast our cupcakes, raise them high,
Let's sprinkle laughter, oh me, oh my!

Tales of Sweet Tidings

In the land of crème brulee dreams,
Chocolate rivers burst at the seams,
Marzipan maps lead the way,
To frosty fun every day!

Twinkling lights and caramel cheers,
Whisking away our worries and fears,
Fudgy stories dance in the air,
Filled with giggles, joy, and flair.

Sprinkling sugar like confetti bright,
With creamy wonders, it feels so right,
Tales of sweetness weave through the night,
In bakery corners, what a delight!

Candy canes curl in a fuzzy embrace,
Making us grin with their candy-laced grace,
Oh, what fun in this sugary play,
With treats and laughter, we'll stay all day!

Enchanted Flavors of the Night

In the air, a scent so sweet,
Gingerbread men tap their feet.
With a wink and a silly grin,
They tango while the night begins.

Marshmallow clouds float up high,
Chasing dreams that giggle and sigh.
Chocolate rivers run right through,
With candy canes that tell you, "Boo!"

Frosted stars twinkle with cheer,
Caramel laughter fills the sphere.
Sprinkles dance on cream so light,
As we munch through the playful night.

Tasty whispers, sweets galore,
Come join the jesting at the door!
With every nibble, laughter's near,
In a world that's sugar and cheer.

A Tapestry of Treats and Wishes

A swirl of colors, bright and bold,
Gumdrops giggle, stories told.
The lollipops are having fun,
Chasing sunbeams, everyone!

Cotton candy clouds drift by,
While jellybeans wave goodbye.
Gingersnap dancers take the floor,
Whisking up chaos, more and more!

Cocoa springs burst with delight,
Splashing joy both day and night.
Merry mischief, frolicsome glee,
Join the feast, come sing with me!

Plum pudding casts a funny spell,
With giggling elves who know it well.
Each joyous bite a silly surprise,
In this banquet of tasty lies!

Satin Soft Whispers of Yuletide

Fluffy whispers on soft snow,
Marzipan skies singing low.
Charming fairies with candy wings,
Around the tree, they spin and sing.

Chuckle cakes with frosted smiles,
Stroll down candy-coated aisles.
Frosty pixies twirl and sway,
Crafting giggles into play.

Nutty nibbles dance in sync,
With jokes that make the eggnog wink.
Each treat wrapped in laughter bright,
Spreading joy, oh, what a sight!

Bubbly sauces, sticky sweet,
Mirthful echoes in the heat.
Satin voices blend with cheer,
Creating mischief, spreading near.

Honeyed Hopes and Frosty Hours

Syrupy dreams on snowy beds,
Giggling snowflakes fill our heads.
Honey drips from frosty beams,
In a world that swirls with schemes.

Waffle cones with ticklish pride,
Hold the giggles that can't hide.
Fuzzle nuts and blueberry sighs,
Materialize as laughter flies.

Frosted marshmallows twist and twirl,
Creating mischief, let it unfurl!
Every nibble, sweet and round,
Spins a tale of joy profound.

Jolly flakes swirl all around,
Wrapping love in frosty sound.
With every chuckle, joy ignites,
As we snack through these merry nights.

Twinkling Lights and Tasty Nights

Under the glow of flickering beams,
Gingerbread men dance like they're in dreams.
Hot cocoa spills on cheerful old sweaters,
Laughter erupts—who needs any letters?

Jingle bells jingle, but crunch goes the snack,
Watch out for crumbs; they're all on your back!
Cookies are tempting, but there's too much dough,
Just one more bite? You really can't say no!

Twinkle and tinkle, the ornaments sway,
Cats knock them down as we shout, "Hooray!"
Eggnog spills over, the cat gives a sigh,
"This holiday cheer is a pie in the eye!"

When bedtime calls, all snug in our beds,
We dream of sweet treats dancing in our heads.
The clock strikes midnight, it's time for a feast,
With mints and giggles, we nibble the least.

Mints and Melodies by the Hearth

By the warm hearth, the stories unfold,
Of sugar cube castles and gummy bears bold.
Tinsel hangs low while candy canes sway,
The dog tries to snatch one, but it's ours, hey!

Caroling echoes, off-key with bright cheer,
A snowman in slippers just begged us to leer.
We sing of the joy that the cold cannot steal,
As our sweet treats keep us spinning like a wheel.

Marshmallow snowmen start melting away,
Stuck in hot cocoa, quite happy to stay.
A sprinkle of laughter, a dash of delight,
This seasonal chaos is pure comic blight!

Singing and snacking till midnight's parade,
With cheeks full of gumdrops, our plans start to fade.
But who could resist such a whimsical show?
Mints and melodies, oh, how they do glow!

Sweets for the Season's Greet

Frosty mornings with a sprinkle of flair,
Stockings lined up, but who put them there?
Taffy and fudge make our hearts skip with glee,
Such sticky situations, oh what a spree!

Giggles abound, while we dive in the stash,
Candy canes crunch, crowned in powdered sugar splash.
Trading our goodies, oh what a swap,
I've got two chocolates if you give me that pop!

Jolly old Santa forgot where he parked,
His sleigh full of treats—who knew he was stark?
Come gather around with a smile on your face,
For 'tis the season to see who's the ace!

Cookies a-plenty, with sprinkles galore,
Each bite is a laugh; we just keep wanting more.
With sweets piled high, we take one last glance,
And dive into merriment, ready to dance!

Frosted Heartstrings and Holiday Hues

Frosting on noses, it's pure holiday cheer,
While snowballs are packed into little kids' gear.
Sleds dashing by, with laughter in tow,
Bright colors of joy in a wintertime show.

Gifts wrapped in ribbons, but cats see the fate,
They leap on the table—it's a sugary state!
With bows and with jingles, we sing out with pride,
These heartstrings of humor are all we can hide.

Chasing our shadows in the sparkling light,
Playing hopscotch with snowflakes till late in the night.
With eggnog in hand, we raise up our cups,
To all silly moments, let's drink from the ups!

As laughter erupts in this festive affair,
Children with wishes, their hearts laid so bare.
With frosting and cheer, we embrace all the views,
In frosted heartstrings and holiday hues!

Milton Keynes UK
Ingram Content Group UK Ltd.
UKHW021350011224
451618UK00023B/230